Praise for Kare's Books

"Kare's incisive techniques have a powerful impact."

—Leigh Steinberg, sports agent

"When it comes to first impressions, Kare is the final word! Read *Resolving Conflict Sooner* and you'll be amazed at what you can learn from Kare, the master of relationships!"

—T. Scott Gross, speaker and author of Borrowed Dreams,
Positively Outrageous Customer Service *and other books*

"I predict grand things for Kare and everyone who practices her techniques."

—Jay Levinson, author of Guerrilla Marketing books

"She'll forever change how you see yourself and your world."

—David Rockefeller, Jr.

"Her methods are so powerful they can make peacekeeping an ingrained daily habit."

—Thelton Henderson, federal judge, U.S. Ninth Circuit Court

"Kare's thoughtful, creative ideas have helped me in all my relationships—personal as well as professional. She'll show you how going through conflict well can actually deepen relationships."

—Janine Warner, Online Managing Editor, Miami Herald

"Her approach to agreement-reaching is a breakthrough technique."

—Roger Dawson, author of The Confident Decisionmaker
and five books on negotiation

Praise continued...

"You can tell whether a person is clever by the way they answer questions. You can tell whether a person is wise by listening to the questions they ask. You can tell if a book has the heart and soul of the author in it when you read the advice they offer. I believe Kare Anderson writes cleverly, wisely and with a dedicated heart and soul."

—*Max Hitchins, past Australian President of National Speakers Association of Australia*

"Oil on troubled waters—that's what Kare's new book spreads. Her 4-step plan transforms discord into accord fast. Her process flows smoothly with the natural rhythms of human nature. It's a true resolution success system."

—*Burt Dubin, creator, Speaking Success System*

"For anyone managing, selling, or working with people, this book is a must read. It will show you how to turn potential conflicts into opportunities for increasing your personal influence and achieving greater business success."

—*Mark D. French, president, Leading Authorities*

"Unbelievable! Kare Anderson has captured the essence of the most powerful strategies for achieving success in overcoming the challenges and difficulties of dealing with people in all aspects of life. These problem solving techniques combined with dispute resolution tactics can improve all aspects of your life—at work with colleagues, employees and management, in business with customers and competitors, and at home with children and parents, and in love and marriage. This is the bible on how to win friends and influence people in the 21st Century."

—*Paul J. Krupin, JD, Founder, Direct Contact/Imediafax*

"In 1873, Sir John Erickson, Surgeon General to Queen Victoria said 'The chest and the brain will forever be shut from the intrusion of the wise and humane surgeon.' Just as surgeons have learned to open the brain and the chest to good effect, Kare Anderson knows how to open the mind and the heart to help everyone work through the difficulties of relationships. Use only sweet words, you may have to eat them, goes an old cowboy saying. Kare Anderson is a gourmand in the kitchen of relationships. She really knows how to combine all the ingredients to produce the most palatable results."

-Tom Morrison, Phoenix Leasing

"Just when I was faced with a delicate situation, along comes Kare Anderson with her special sort of clear, concrete insights. Kare delivers practical advice for resolving conflict that anyone can use by tapping into inherent abilities, and she presents it in an accessible—and adoptable—framework. After learning these invaluable techniques, I'll go into my next meeting with a clearer sense of how everyone can come out ahead and feel great about the outcome!"

—Mary Westheimer, President, BookZone.com

"You don't learn the real substance of organizations from the lines in books. It is between the lines. In her new book, Kare captures moments that fall in between the lines. Her remedies are practical and valuable to anyone hoping to communicate positively everyday."

—Pat Christenson, Director, Thomas & Mack Center and Sam Boyd Stadium

"Kare's techniques changed how I face every interaction."

—Elaine College, Vice President, Busch Gardens Entertainment

Praise continued...

"As a lawyer who often negotiates on behalf of a large public institution, Kare reminds me of the initial urges and instincts I need to understand and resist. Each of her steps are ones that I quickly recognize in my most successful adversaries."

— *Mike Smith, legal counsel, UC Berkeley*

"Kare never ceases to amaze me in her constant ability to provide useful tips and info to help and guide me through many personal and business relationships."

— *Chris McClean, Pertinent Information Ltd.*

"Here are the inside secrets to communicating with anyone— even those people who get on your nerves and disagree with everything you say! Kare is a master at communicating under any situation. At last we have her tested wisdom in one very cool book. Get it! Read it! Memorize it!"

— *Joe Vitale, marketing specialist, author of* There's A Customer Born Every Minute: P. T. Barnum's Secrets to Business Success

"Convert enemies into allies and turn disagreements into harmonious interactions with Kare's new discord diminishing book, *Resolving Conflict Sooner.* Kare shows us that the pathway to resolving conflict is simple, easy and effective when we first become honest with ourselves. I have experienced tremendous fulfillment, joy and peace in all my business and personal relationships by using the simple steps that Kare has outlined in this well-timed masterpiece."

— *Allen D'Angelo, M.S., author of* Power Pacing and Fun, Creative & Profitable Salon Marketing

Resolving Conflict
Sooner

The powerfully simple 4-step method for
reaching better agreements more easily in
everyday life

Kare Anderson

THE CROSSING PRESS
FREEDOM, CALIFORNIA

For information on bulk purchases or group discounts for this
and other Crossing Press titles, please contact our Special Sales
Manager at 800/777-1048.
Visit our web site at: www.crossingpress.com

Library of Congress Cataloging-in-Publication Data

Anderson, Kare.
    Resolving conflict sooner / by Kare Anderson.
        p. cm.
    ISBN 0-89594-976-8
    1. Interpersonal conflict. 2. Conflict management.
    3. Conflict (Psychology) I. Title.
    BF637.I48A55 1999
    303.6'9—dc21   98-56511
                                                    CIP

Contents

What would improve your happiness more than being able to resolve more conflict smoothly, with less angst?

. . . .

Imagine seeing yourself forging agreements sooner and feeling genuinely satisfied with the solution.

. . . .

Imagine seeing the other person also satisfied.

. . . .

Imagine seeing both of you secure in the knowledge that the agreement will hold and you will not have to go through the conflict again.

Preface

Here's a paradox of apparently opposite emotional truths: the expression of both affection and anger spark similar turning points in the delicate nature of relationships, for it is often not our intent but the manner in which we offer or receive the emotion that determines the result. Our perceptions, actions, and reactions are never, never neutral. After conflict we either back off or move closer together.

Perhaps that's why the way you handle conflict holds the key to your ability to connect with others. I hope this book helps you move closer towards cultivating more genuine, enduring relationships.

Understanding Conflict

What is conflict? It's when two or more people take different and opposing positions in a situation, expressed verbally or in actions. Either way, the conflict starts when one person feels his interests are threatened by the other person. It begins with these two individuals and then spreads to groups which those people are part of—families, companies, civic groups, religious communities, political groups, any kind of organization. More people will come to believe they have something at stake in the conflict and therefore must take a side. And suddenly the fabric that holds people together, that connects them, is at risk. Once feelings have hardened, the chances are radically diminished that a resolution can occur. Therefore, it is very important to stop the acceleration of the conflict before it escalates into more people on each side.

There is a pivotal point when you can have the most influence over the way the conflict will go. You can take two roads. The first road will be quite rocky, presenting obstacles which you yourself have created. The second will be much smoother, because you will have become conscious of those potential obstacles. It's that early, generally overlooked, pivotal point when you will have the most influence over which way a conflict will go.

This is the point where you can escalate the conflict or refuse to do so.

There are two kinds of pain: pain of risk and pain of regret.

With all the material available on conflict, we seldom discuss the importance of the precise time the conflict begins and the crucial pivotal point that occurs almost instantly afterwards. Conflict begins when the difference in two people's positions first becomes apparent to one person. It may become apparent because of a comment, an action, or even an omission of a comment or an action, but it is always with that first notion that one person views another as an adversary.

Rarely do two people simultaneously recognize a difference in positions or interests. The second person will know it soon thereafter. That first person usually has the greatest opportunity to influence whether the conflict will escalate and harden. He has a choice. That choice, more than any other action he will take, will fundamentally influence his ability to find satisfaction in the situation. In that pivotal moment he can turn in one of two directions. It should be understood that there are no neutral actions, especially when our antennae are up in anticipation of a fight.

A lot happens in those first few moments when one person realizes the possibility of loss—every conflict represents a perceived potential loss of some kind. He can lower his energy in an attempt to foster a positive response to the other person. He can become open and act in an open manner so that he can find a compromise as things unfold. On the other hand, he can close up and look for more signs of disagreement. He can stop looking for signs of good will and agreement. His attitude and action can set the tone and influence the situation, the rules by which they will engage in discussion, and the tempo of the action.

Actually, some apparent differences can be resolved even before the other person realizes there is a conflict. The first person can choose to observe the situation coolly, looking for ways to settle the matter without engaging the other person in discussion. The second person in the situation can also use that pivotal point to stay open, even if the first person has already acted, but the second person's actions will have less effect in the situation.

Suppose you are that first person to experience a conflict arising. You feel vulnerable and instinctively put your guard up. Ironically that reaction will make you even more vulnerable. Because you are signaling that your position is weak, you are unwittingly guiding the energy of the ensuing disagreement to your most vulnerable areas. That is why, in that pivotal moment, your choice towards remaining open serves not only to move you toward eventual resolution, but also to protect you. You will be less of a target and attract less escalation toward conflict, because you will be acting as if the conflict won't occur. You will appear more safe to others in the situation, and you will maintain more options, including the option to escalate later on. Instead of following your natural instinct to look for more bad signs and prepare to defend yourself or retaliate, you will find it natural to stay aware and open. You will then gain more information about the situation and more insight into the motivation and real meaning of the other person's actions.

In that moment when you first experience the body prickle of heat remember that reward. It won't be easy, but it will be easier than the alternatives. Once you've practiced it you will know what I am saying is true. Power flows towards you when you use the pivotal point to try to make peace. Hard as it may be to believe right now, your conscious choice to do this will eventually become habitual over time.

This book is about the steps you can take to resolve conflict when you feel that hot prickle of awareness that means a conflict is imminent. You will learn a four-step method that you can use to gain more pleasure and less pain out of your daily interactions. Make your pledge now to read and start practicing with the next person you encounter so you can experience the difference in your life patterns.

> Say what you want others to hear only after they have seen what they need to see in you.

Humans, like all animals, express their anger through body language (eye-pupil dilation, skin temperature, hostile gestures). Such reactions beget a mirrored response from the presumed enemy, and the intensity of the conflict increases exponentially.

Note that while we are doing this, we justify our own behavior and find no justification for the other person's behavior. Rather than first determining what the other side wants, we talk about what we want. Consequently, neither party feels that it is being heard. Each party describes what divides the two parties rather than what connects them. Each party talks from a perspective of "me" or "us" to "you," causing even more resistance. It's a face-off, leading either to withdrawal with resentment on one side and righteousness on the other side, or attack on both sides. Everyone loses in the long run.

> Failure is usually no more fatal than success is permanent.

Because we are stuck in a mode of unconscious reacting rather than consciously choosing to act, we often do not first ask ourselves what is truly in our own best interest. This is especially true in an emotionally charged relationship. If we don't really care about another person, if the emotional stakes are low, we can resolve a conflict more easily. When the stakes are higher, we generally exhibit destructive patterns, and the further we get into a conflict, the longer it will take to reach a solution. Moreover, there will be lingering bad feelings about the experience in everyone involved.

Are you ready to choose a smoother path? Would you like to learn an easy process to prevent conflicts from escalating? There is a solution. You can take a four-step roundtrip through conflict, coming back to yourself after it's all over, feeling proud and satisfied both with the result and the relationship.

You yourself are the source of conflict as well as the source of the resolution to conflict. You are responsible for the entire trip. And the way you handle conflict holds the key to the way you will feel about yourself, your pride and your self-respect. If you are puzzled about the last conflict you found yourself in, you might find these questions useful.

After the Next Conflict, I Don't Want To

1. Feel defeated, hostile, resentful, vindictive, hurt, or otherwise powerless.

2. Feel like a jerk or a negative person.

3. Feel drained of the energy I could otherwise devote to positive, life-affirming tasks and relationships.

4. Make an enemy who could cause me trouble in the future.

5. Continue the same self-defeating script of fighting with people who will of necessity remain in my life.

6. Go through more self-defeating conflicts in my life.

After the Next Conflict, I Do Want To

1. Like myself afterwards because I know I have shown my power in a positive, not a negative way.

2. Like my opponent afterwards, or at least feel I can say hello when I meet them on the street.

3. Feel that the conflict reached an appropriate closure or that I reached my own closure and therefore could move on with my life.

4. Give my own time and energy to positive tasks and relationships from which I could draw energy.

5. Create new "scripts" with people whom I love and want in my life, as well as with difficult people whom I can't for various reasons dislodge from my life.

6. Have less worry and more fun in my life.

The Roundtrip

In conflict we usually get more clear and also more intense about what we don't want, rather than what we do want. We simply react—we don't choose how we want to act. By so doing, we give our power away by letting others determine our behavior. It's always more productive to be proactive, to see how you can clear the air. The benefits to both parties are obvious: if it's a relationship you wish to continue, you can do so; if it isn't, you can at least be civil to the people whenever you meet them. You haven't created an enemy.

I know it is difficult to reach an agreement when tension is rising, but if you follow these four steps, it is easier to reach a resolution to conflict than any alternative I have found. If you are serious about wanting to change your method of operating in the world, please memorize and practice these four steps every day in the low-level conflicts that will arise frequently in your office, in your manufacturing plant, in your home. These little deals can escalate into full-blown conflicts that will leave lifelong scars if you don't react appropriately. With a Roundtrip, you can salvage the relationship, even though it may not seem worthwhile in the heat of the moment.

If you steady yourself and decide to be active rather than reactive, you will be proud and satisfied with the results and the ensuing relationships. It's an accomplishment that is well worth the effort.

> You often don't know what you don't know. Get the facts, or the facts will get you.

The following is a brief summary of the four steps. They are explored more fully later on in the book.

Step One—Tell Yourself the Truth

We humans build a wall around ourselves, a defense system that clicks into operation whenever we feel affronted in any way. In a moment of confrontation, either real or imagined, we escalate into the hottest negative reaction we can summon. At such moments, we need to slow down the process and seek personal clarity by asking the important question: What do we want? What's our bottom line?

Step Two—Reach Out to the Other Side

Ask yourself these questions. What is the other person's greatest need? What is most important to them? These questions are particularly important if the other side doesn't know their greatest need.

> Beliefs shape our experience, not the other way around.

Step Three—Listen Attentively to the Other Side

Listen to the other person and demonstrate to that person that you have heard their concerns. Proper respect must be shown at all times. You must mean it. Attitude and words must be respectful and responsive. Power plays will not work at this stage, or later on for that matter. This is often the most crucial time in a conflict, when your actions can either spark escalation or initiate a cooling off period. Don't rush or push now. The more you dislike the other side, the more time and effort you must summon to prove that you are indeed listening, that you are aware of their needs.

Step Four—Prove You Are Fair

When you propose a solution, prove that you are fair, by addressing the other person's interests first. Describe, in their language, how he can benefit. Then you can discuss the benefits of such a resolution to yourself as well. This is a way of showing proper respect.

It's important to keep this Roundtrip in your mind and to use it frequently in every skirmish that arises on the path to resolution. A Roundtrip will work because it teaches you how to go slow in order to go fast. What seems like an agonizingly slow process will prove to be a fast lane to resolution. Please spend enough time to get clear about the two most important factors at every stage in the conflict: your most important need and the other person's most important need.

By taking the time (the first two steps of the Roundtrip), you will get centered and accumulate the information necessary to formulate the correct approach to the situation. Then and only then, you can move more quickly. The beginning of a conflict is the time to become sure of what you are doing, to slow yourself down to the point where you can be honest about yourself and empathic about the other person.

After these two steps, you will find yourself calm and poised. You will know the other person's hot buttons, ɯotivations, needs. What are they protecting? What is their image? What is causing them to be aggressive? What will make them feel better? By doing this work, you will be present, not locked behind your own wall. This will enable the other side to drop their defenses as well.

Here's an oval diagram you can use as a visual anchor. Use it to keep calm and on track with the four steps to resolution, no matter what the circumstances. Don't let the other side trigger a response from you. You and only you will choose how you will behave.

Don't bypass any one of the four steps on your trip. Move from confusion and overreaction to clarity and

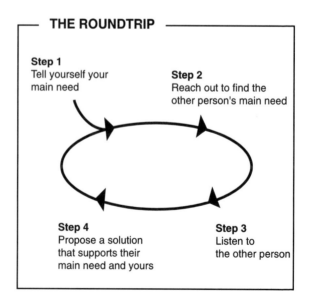

THE ROUNDTRIP

Step 1
Tell yourself your main need

Step 2
Reach out to find the other person's main need

Step 4
Propose a solution that supports their main need and yours

Step 3
Listen to the other person

serenity, from negative feelings about the other side to solid connections with them. When you see tension looming, keep your own truth in mind.

Refer to the oval image as you go through a day, use it as your main reference point, your context, your bottom line. Use it to help you stay centered and receptive. See the oval as a never-ending path to your positive connection to other people and ultimately to your own happiness.

Each Roundtrip will give you an opportunity to learn how times of conflict can actually bring people closer, instead of tearing them apart. With such practice, your path through life can grow less bumpy.

> In a civilization where love is gone, we turn to justice. When justice is gone, we turn to power. And when power is gone, we turn to violence.

Ten Ways Roundtrips Can Be Useful

1. Roundtrips can be applied to any situation: at home, at work—in any public or private situation.

2. Because you have a method to use in times of conflict, you will more likely be active rather than reactive. You can choose your actions consciously.

3. Roundtripping, because it is clear, brief, and easy to use, can become a healthy habit.

4. Because it has only four steps, you can easily practice it, making it an instinctive response.

5. Roundtripping is based on honesty and mutual support, not on lies or power over.

6. Because it enables you to stay balanced, it will prevent you from being aggressive and attacking the other side, or from becoming passive and backing off from a confrontation.

7. Because it is based on work on yourself, it offers you a route with detours, but no dead ends.

8. Your actions will be drawn from your authentic self, compelling others to present their most genuine selves.

9. Roundtripping makes for better agreements that people are more motivated to keep.

10. You choose consciously how you wish to act and be seen in the world.

Ten Ways You Can Stop a Conflict from Escalating

1. By thinking about your own needs in Step One, you zero out the resentment of the other side. Essentially, since you no longer will consider them the enemy, you have curbed their resentment.

2. A Roundtrip helps you main your objectivity. It's far more difficult to resolve conflicts when you have strong emotions about the other person.

3. Since Step One requires you to identify your own need first, it eliminates the natural frustration you would feel in not knowing what you want.

4. By taking the time for Step Two, you slow down the pace of the discussion. Rushing the beginning of a relationship often makes the other person shut down.

5. Step Two also helps you avoid the easy assumption that the same kind of offer works for every person and situation.

6. Step Two prevents you from being overpowering, thus preventing the other person's natural antagonism from increasing.

7. By speaking first to the other person's needs in Step Three, you demonstrate that you have placed their needs above yours, and you therefore avoid appearing selfish and unfair.

Ten Ways You Can Stop a Conflict from Escalating
continued

8. With Step Three, you do not appear to be an antagonist. It's an approach that will help heal the situation.

9. With Step Three, you are more likely to propose solutions the other person can accept because you have given yourself more time to recognize what they want most and want most to avoid. You make fewer untested assumptions about the other person's needs and desires. Consequently, you will not appear oblivious or thoughtless.

10. In summary, by taking a Roundtrip, you will always be able to find the best mutual interest, even if you are given a very short time to make a decision.

Step One

Identify Your Main Need

Like cutting up different ingredients before you turn on the stove to cook a Chinese stir-fry, if you spend more prep time considering your bottom line for resolution of the conflict, the stir-frying, *i.e.*, the action, will flow more quickly and easily.

Knowing what you want also enables you to be more in control of yourself and therefore more relaxed. Moreover, when you know this bottom line before going into a situation, you have a context for the discussion. The table is not empty—there's food on it. You can be more open and flexible, a better listener. Without a context you are more likely to react rather than to act, perhaps ignoring your main need.

In advance, ask yourself, "What do I most need?" "What result is most important to me here? If I had complete control over the outcome, what would it be?"

When you increase the preliminary work, you increase your chances for success.

Make "What Do I Want" an Automatic Response

Challenging situations will always arise—that's just part of life, but when your automatic response to anyone's behavior is, "How does this relate to my bottom line?" you become clearer sooner about what you want to do. And you will maintain this clarity more frequently in future occasions and thus become less reactive and consequently more powerful. Paradoxically, the more selfish you are about knowing what's important to you, the more selfless you can be. You can hear and serve another person's needs in ways that work for you both.

To know what you want, be specific, then get even more specific. Children are clearer and more specific about their needs than adults, so try to think like a child. What would a satisfactory solution look like? Can you describe it in detail: what time of day, what surroundings? What person would do what, feel what, get what? How and when would a satisfactory solution take place? How would the other person feel about himself, about the entire situation? How would that outcome affect your life? Would it be the same, better, worse than it is now? Would the short-term effect be different from the long-term effect?

How would you perceive yourself if you were able to achieve the specific solution you imagine? Would you feel proud? How would others perceive you? Would the solution bring you closer to the other person, or would it separate you from them and other people as well?

Our Survival Instinct Works Against Us

Our survival instinct wires us to respond more quickly to the sense of danger than it does to the thrill of opportunity. We respond more quickly with negative reactions than with positive reactions, and these negative reactions last for a much longer time than positive reactions. When we respond to perceived danger, we think in very general terms about what we want, whereas our feelings are much stronger about what we don't want. When you focus on the rock in the road ahead, you're more likely to hit it.

> The long way around a Roundtrip often results in a shorter route than the straight-line offensive.

Consider Alternatives and Choose One

Life is very often a series of trade-offs. The more options you can picture in any situation, the more likely you will be satisfied with the one you choose. Usually, more options are available early in a discussion before conflict escalates or the pressure of time builds up. Make a list of your alternatives with their possible consequences. Prioritize these as a way to make your first choice.

Increase your advance preparation time and increase your chances for success.

Create an Image of Your Bottom Line Need in One Sentence

Be concrete and specific about what you want.

1. Exactly what will the result look like?
2. How will it make me feel?
3. What details will make it more real?

Create a vivid mental picture of the result and define it precisely in one sentence. The shorter it is, the clearer your purpose will be, the greater capacity you will have to attract agreement. The following sentence is too vague to be effective: "I want the other person to be more cooperative." This sentence will be effective: "I want the other person to work on these specific tasks on a joint project."

Know Yourself and What Is Important to You

Most people make choices without being fully conscious about what motivates them. The better you know yourself, the better able you will be to make good choices. Please answer the following questions.

1. What and whom do you most value?
2. What do you want to be remembered for?
3. What makes you happy?
4. What life changes must you make and when?
5. How do you spend your time and money?
6. What most excites you?
7. What most upsets you?
8. When you find yourself irritated by a certain person, can you find out why?
9. When you find yourself admiring a certain person, do you know why?

How Do Others Perceive You?

With a clear vision of who you are, your choices, personal or professional, become more effortless and less complicated. You will have a reference point from which you can always make your choices. Now that you know how to perceive yourself, check your assumptions about how other people see you. Please answer the following questions:

1. What are the main reasons you like and admire yourself?

2. Why do people like and admire you—the main reasons?

3. What is your main attribute that draws people to you?

4. What is your main attribute that repels people?

5. What are other people's situations, behaviors, personality traits that most irritate you?

6. What do other people believe are the main reasons you get upset?

To be seen by other people the same way we see ourselves is rare. Conflicts therefore often arise from the difference between our perceptions of ourselves and other people's perceptions. To be able to see ourselves as others see us is a complicated process.

Understand Your Patterns of Behavior

Please consider any of your patterns of recurring conflict. Look over your past life, even the past month, perhaps with your personal calendar in hand, to see patterns in the conflicts you have experienced. Can you step to a higher plane of behavior?

Take for instance driving your car. Do you ever drive defensively by looking two or three cars ahead so that you can anticipate trouble before it happens? Can you similarly look ahead of your present situation in an attempt to avoid potential trouble? How can you stop any process which might result in conflict?

What Are Your Sources of Power?

You can start by recognizing before a conflict arises where you have resources, where you will find support and comfort? Please go through your list of family, affinity group, friends, colleagues, and so on, to see whom you can count on to help you. Who are the people who can't help you? Where and how can you attract more people to help you, perhaps different people from those you have around you presently?

If you focus on the rock in the road ahead, you are more likely to hit it.

On the other hand, how are you supporting your friends in their time of difficulty? What talents do you have in this direction? How can you improve these talents? How can you deepen the connection between yourself and other people? In what kind of conflicts, with whom, and in what circumstances, are you in most need of support? And who would be most helpful to you, in what ways and times?

If you give other people what they need in their lives, you often get what you need in return, perhaps before you even knew you needed such support. It may even come from sources you didn't even know you had.

"A belligerent beginning is seldom overcome."

Ikaku Masao,
martial arts expert

Step Two

What Are the Other Person's Needs?

Now that you've completed Step One and established your bottom line, focus on what is most important to the other party involved in the conflict. This process may be clouded by conscious or unconscious beliefs you may have about them.

For example, you were probably taught to show disagreement a certain way. How is it appropriate to respond to people who show disagreement differently? Similarly, you probably have internalized beliefs about other people, based on their appearance, profession, demeanor, etc. Is it possible that these assumptions may lead you to form inaccurate assumptions about these people?

Try to see situations through their eyes, and listen to what they say carefully. Are your assumptions about them and what they really want correct?

Remember that beliefs shape our experience, not the other way around.

Defensive Driving: The Look Ahead Rule

What will you do the next time a person acts in a way that annoys you? Can you look ahead to such a situation and anticipate what you would do? Before you meet the people with whom you are in conflict, please take the time to look ahead and ask yourself these questions.

1. What will you do?
2. How will the other person react?
3. How will you respond to this?
4. How will the other person react to you?
5. What will you do then?
6. What will the other person do then?
7. What will you do then?

I am saying something simple here: action begets reaction.

What Do the Other Side's Words and Behavior Mean?

Everyone has a personal set of assumptions about what certain words and actions mean, though they may not be aware of these assumptions. Two people may do or say the same thing, but with totally different intentions.

Conversely, two people may do or say completely different things, but with the same intention.

You have to set aside your own assumptions first. Then, by examining what they do or say very carefully, you will come to understand what threatens or pleases them, and you will get a notion of their bottom line.

When you are trying to establish this, do avoid asking questions that seem to be an attempt to justify your own behavior, or seem to be an attempt to gain ground. Ask questions that will help you ascertain who they are.

Look to others' positive intentions, especially when they appear to have none, not for their benefit, but for yours.

Recognize and Try to Discard Your Fears

We fuel our fears by assuming thinking they are exactly what the other side intends to do. Don't try to deduce other people's intentions from your own fears. Conflicts make everybody feel afraid, and it is natural to suppose that the other side will do the things we fear most.

Realize that everybody holds both conscious and unconscious fears. You will first have to acknowledge these fears and then put them aside. It's necessary to do this in order to listen openly to the other person and respond in a wholehearted fashion. It's hard to acknowledge others when you are dreading the worst or feeling powerless, or making false assumptions about their motives. By putting aside your own fears, you'll be helping the other side do it too, and you will then be more receptive to each other.

When you know nobody can take from you what is really yours, you stop trying to protect it.

To use the Roundtrip, each participant must have the commitment and method to understand the other party's wiring and then speak in a style that's comfortable for them so that they will feel more comfortable and open with you.

Try to See the World the Way Other People Do

Don't assume that you know what another person wants, even if you know that other person well. Similarly, don't presume that you know what other people mean from what they say. Ask them what they mean before you act, and ask again to confirm your understanding of what they say. As a third step, tell them what you thought you heard them say. Our most inaccurate communication is often with people with whom we have strong feelings, the ones we love or hate. Take time and special care in such cases to validate your assumptions before acting on them.

Just as you have identified your own assumptions, motivations, and prejudices, you should try to identify the other party's assumptions, motivations, and prejudices.

1. What excites them?
2. What bores them?
3. What frightens them?
4. Who rewards and penalizes them for what?
5. How are they rewarded or penalized?
6. What do they want most from life, specifically from people they know?
7. How do they spend their time and money?
8. Who are their heroines and heroes?
9. What are their goals?
10. What actions do they judge wrong or right?

You can never really know anyone until you see the choices they make. We all go through life assuming our own viewpoint is the only true or right way. If you don't look like another person or act like another person, the harder it is for that person to hear you at all, even though you are cooperating fully. You don't look "right," i.e., like them. All people have trouble hearing another person until that person becomes familiar, until they can see points of similarity. Familiarity often breeds acceptance—some kind of commonality is necessary before people will hear each other.

Look for other people's blind spots or hot buttons. This can be helpful in two ways. By becoming more aware of their hot buttons, you will find out that they are not conscious of these. Because very few people like to have their blind spots pointed out to them, don't use that knowledge to correct them. Use it to anticipate trouble and to skirt it. When you know their hot buttons better than they do, you are less likely to be surprised by their outbursts.

As you fix the problem, you won't need to fix the blame.

Step Three

People Like People Who Are Like Them

People are slower to feel comfortable around others who do not look "right" to them. In fact, the research reveals that we have trouble hearing each other initially, even during the most genial interactions. We narrow our peripheral vision in the presence of unfamiliar people or unfamiliar surroundings. Only when we feel safe do we literally open up to see and hear the other person. We feel more at ease with people we can more readily understand, those people who are like us. We are more apt to read another person's visual and verbal cues accurately. These clues are the person's appearance, action, tone, and words.

We react most strongly to people who are obviously different from us in age, ethnicity, gender, and size. There is a secondary level of differences that will also increase the chances that we will misunderstand each other. These include religious, moral, and political beliefs; the economic level in which we were raised or to which we are now accustomed; the profession and industry in which we work. Also it will matter whether we are parents; married or single; in robust health or not; shy or outgoing; physically or mentally disabled; are currently under great stress or not; or have experienced a recent loss or a wonderful new beginning.

These differences will present you with a risk and an opportunity. Your appearance, words, and actions can more easily be misinterpreted by the other side in a conflict. This is the risk when you speak to a person whose appearance, words, and actions are different from yours. However, you are granted an opportunity at the same time. You may gain new skills that will be useful.

To experience the benefits, when interacting with someone who is different from you, spend more time with Step Two and move slowly in order to build trust from the first. Invest more time in demonstrating good will. You also have the opportunity to see the world through a stranger's eyes and discover how that person likes to be treated, a crucial piece of knowledge as you move forward during the conflict. Bring out the part of you that is most like the other person, and demonstrate that part of you in how you speak, appear, and move.

Do not attempt to emulate the other person in dress or actions if these actions are not true to you. Spend a longer time confirming the areas of agreement. Seek their suggestions earlier about how to move toward a mutually satisfying agreement. If you have misread the person, be honest and admit it. Ask for their guidance if you misinterpret their words, assuring them that you will do the same. Your forthright acknowledgment of the obvious differences and your honestly stated intent to learn from the situation can put the differences on the table for the other person to acknowledge or not. Prove your commitment to acting in good faith by being authentic in your language and consistent in seeking their perspective early on. Reinforce your need to spend more time getting to know them and building trust by reminding yourself of two potential payoffs.

Supplant your fears with greater motivation.

1. This is a rich opportunity to build a relationship that can teach you more about the world.

2. This will develop your skills in connecting and communicating with people who are different from you. This is a skill that will make you more valuable to others, in that they can learn to emulate you.

> You never really know someone until you see the choices they make.

You may not only come to an agreement with this person who is different from you.

1. You may glean insights into facets of yourself as you stretch to make connection in new ways.

2. You can build an enduring relationship with someone who brings out new sides of you, and who can help you see the world in a new light.

3. Strengthen your ability to get along with diverse others. You may, in fact, attract positive power as you become the safe center in a skirmish among people who are different than each other.

Even if you don't wind up liking each other, work towards the goal of establishing a mutual trust so that both sides can afford to act in good faith, despite the differences. Ironically, this slower path towards trust may build a deeper trust over time.

Allow Time to Get in Sync

Gypsy Rose Lee used to say, "Anything worth doing is worth doing slowly." When you are beginning to establish a connection, in order to build feelings of safety and rapport, do less rather than more. Especially at first, control your voice, body movement, position in the room, and posture. Go slow now to go faster later on.

1. Speak in a low-pitched voice. Speak slowly. Don't talk a lot. Less is better than more.
2. Move slowly and make fewer movements. Avoid using your hands a lot.
3. Find a comfortable way of sitting and standing so that you feel and act more comfortable.
4. Practice a body smile of overall geniality. Realize that when you cross your arms over your chest, or cross your legs, you are not letting other people in. Be careful to appear open.

Even fast-paced people don't like to be hurried, especially when they are talking. Don't try to wrap up a discussion quickly; the others may find this suspicious, thinking you're trying to pull a fast one over on them. If this happens, you may have to start from scratch to make them less suspicious. Remember, your aim is to be in sync with them.

You are capable of a wide range of behaviors. The more possible behaviors you have at your disposal, the more options you have to present yourself in a way that makes other people comfortable. Try to look, sound, and move like the other people. Shut people out and they shut up—bring people in and they open up.

A positive outlook attracts other people. Moreover, positive energy creates positive energy—it can bring out their sunnier side. It's a paradox. If you can make yourself believe the world is going to treat you well and focus on those signals, you are more likely to have the world treat you well. Look to people's positive intentions, especially when they appear to be otherwise disposed. You will benefit, even though they may not.

Ask Questions

Remember Columbo, the TV detective? He had a knack for letting others initiate conversations. It's an effective tactic to begin by asking general questions to make everyone feel comfortable, view you as empathic, and give you information quickly.

Try to step into the other person's shoes to see what they are seeing. Try nodding and leaning forward during the parts of the discussion that most relate to your bottom line. Ask for the other person's help so that you can work together to find a solution.

Seek frequent confirmation, input, direction, and feedback. The more opportunities you provide for others to participate in finding a solution, the more likely they will stay with you to find a solution ultimately.

The Important Questions

Now that you have the larger picture, confirm your assumptions by asking the five questions every journalism student is taught: who, what, where, when, why. Then add the how. Start with indirect general questions and work your way toward more specific ones. Indirect, oblique inquiries could include the following.

> Prepare to spend more time and effort staying calm and checking assumptions with those people for whom you have strong feelings of love or hate.

1. What do you think of this situation?

2. How is it affecting you?

3. Have you any suggestions about how to solve this problem?

4. What would make this situation better for you?

Then move to the specific questions.

1. What changes would make this proposal work for you?

2. What do you think we should do before we leave here today?

Remember Columbo? He asks other folks for advice, not because he really needs help, but because he wants to find out what they are really like. He also wants to make them feel more comfortable so that they will be willing to participate in the inquiry.

> The single best sentence for building rapport is, "Tell me more about that."

Ask Advice and Send up Trial Balloons

Speculate out loud. Say, for example, "What if we did so and so?" This sets the direction in which you want the other side to proceed. Asking for advice helps you in several ways: you will get a more complete picture; you will appear to be a willing participant in the solution; and the other person will naturally become more involved.

This approach works particularly well when you are just starting to talk. It also will work when negotiations are stalled and you want to move in a new direction. In brief, get the facts, or the facts will get you.

Paraphrase their comments to confirm you heard them correctly. Make sounds to show you are involved. Sounds expressing approval are wonderful to show that you are involved. Realize when I say sounds I don't mean words, just sounds which tell the speaker that you like what the say.

Listen!

It's smarter to listen than it is to talk—you will have a better chance of gaining rapport. Realize that you don't want to be admired—you want to settle the conflict. Shut up more often, leaving space after other people talk. This will show them they are being heard and respected, also to help them stay grounded. Then, when you are ready to respond, pause for a second or two before you begin in order to make the other side feel more valued. The best single sentence for building rapport is, "Tell me more about that."

Don't Play King of the Mountain

Trying to set the agenda or to take initial charge of the situation sets you up as king of the mountain. It conveys verbally or more often nonverbally that you have all the answers and all the power, that you know what's best for everyone, that you are going to make sure that the right thing happens, that the other people involved are inferior to you, weak, stupid, passive, or easily manipulated. Do so and the other people in the room will naturally resist you in order to maintain their sense of pride and autonomy. Remember that when you give power away, you become more powerful.

It may be instinctive for you to point out the other side's errors, but it is far better to talk first about what you appreciate about the other side. That way you are likely to receive more of what you like. Do try in general to bring out the best in others. People want to act in ways they are perceived positively and any reinforcement you offer them moves the situation along correctly. Do what you can to help them be the best they can be.

With some people you can speak concisely and directly, either because it's their preference or because you instinctively connect and you know they will be comfortable with whatever way you proceed. With most people, however, it will take time before they feel comfortable and open up sufficiently to state what they want. When working with such people, don't try to be a mind reader. Ask them what they most want or need. And even if they evade the question, you can learn more about who they really are from their reaction.

At some point, if you need to talk to other person directly, try this approach. Ask them how they would like to proceed to get this thing resolved soon. Ask them for their thoughts on a solution that would benefit everyone.

It's strange but people reveal far more by their questions than by their answers. If you allow the other person to ask three questions without interrupting them, by the third question the person will be close to expressing their real concerns and interests and perhaps reveal more about themselves than they consciously intend.

Don't invite challenge and competition by taking over. Give away power in order to keep it.

The second part of Step Two is making others feel heard, but this doesn't mean listening to them and dismissing them as stupid or simply wrong. It means truly hearing them and respecting what they have to say. Your assumptions about them will not be hidden—they will know where you stand.

Don't say words like *but* or *however*. These words show that you are disagreeing with them. Your intention should be to make them come closer, not to push them away. Even when (especially when) you don't respect the other person, you must be very careful about your choice of words. You must try to be appear open and respectful.

Your ability to move from the first two steps to Step Three depends on your finding a common ground and getting accurate information. Phrases such as, "You can't really want that," or "I'm sure you must really mean..." indicate that your really don't respect the other person. Start from the reality of where the other person really is, not where you wish them to be.

> **Start from the reality of where others are, not from where you want them to be.**

Control Your Emotions

Don't let emotions sabotage your attempt to forge agreement. Most of the first resolutions to conflict break down because of negative feelings, not because of actual differences over issues or a solution. Before anyone is willing to take Step Four, the situation can fester and remain unresolved because one or more persons is comfortable with the situation remaining precisely the way it is, unresolved.

Why is that so? The reason is simple—we would rather live with the familiar, the ongoing conflict, than with the unfamiliar, the unknown territory, where one person may propose a solution that another may knock down. We are more often afraid of an unknown little loss, such as appearing weak, dumb, or somehow inadequate, than we are motivated to work toward a big improvement in our lives.

Avoid negative reactions such as "That's ridiculous." Such statements shut people down and make them distrust your proposals. They will listen less attentively, and look for ways to prove you wrong. Keep cool under fire. When emotions are hot, create a bridge, not a gulf.

When you feel angry or threatened, you may begin talking faster and at a higher pitch, or you may interrupt the other side. Be careful, talk more slowly, use fewer words, soften your hard edge. When you are tempted to disagree or move too fast, use the four A's.

1. Acknowledge what the other party has just said.

2. Ask for more information.

3. Agree with a part of what the other person has said, or with their positive intent.

4. Add your own view.

Take pains to acknowledge other people's concerns. It may be uncomfortable to speak about their concerns, especially if they have not raised them first, but it is necessary to bring these up in order to reach agreement. Be tactful. Why not say, "If this is your primary concern,..." This may make it easier for the other side to broach the subject themselves directly. Concerns tend to dissipate when they are acknowledged, even if they are not corroborated.

When there is strong rapport or little difference in positions, general acknowledgment may suffice. A simple nod may be sufficient. Visible good will is the strongest persuasion strategy. More intense conflicts require more explicit acknowledgments. In these cases you will be better off if you work harder and longer to build a bridge of trust. You must not forget to use the other person's language and points of reference. And you must not forget to mirror the other person's values, ideas, and words. If you use your own language, they might feel you are twisting their words around or that you simply did not hear them correctly.

Before you move on to Step Four give yourself a progress report. Take a minute to savor your progress. Make sure you know what you want and what the other side wants. Make sure that the other person has felt heard.

By taking Step One you gained clarity and confidence, set a calm, positive tone for your interaction, and helped others become more relaxed in your presence.

By taking Step Two you deepened your connection with the other person and they are more willing to listen to your ideas and talk openly. What's next?

People are far more revealing by the questions they ask than the answers they give.

Step Four

You will need to speak to the other person's needs, values, and self-image. These are the top four complaints people have about their jobs:

1. They don't think people listen to them.
2. They don't feel respected.
3. They think that other people are trying to manipulate or control them.
4. They are not allowed to give input into decisions that affect their work.

You are likely to trigger one of these complaints when you speak to your own needs first. Instead of creating a straight line of opposition in a "me/us"-"you," dialogue, when you take a Roundtrip, you will alleviate these complaints and draw people in. People will then become more motivated to keep the agreements they make.

Begin by talking about a solution that will help them and then proceed to a solution that will help both of you. End with a solution that will help you.

1. Address their needs first.
   (This solution helps you.)

2. Our shared needs next.
   (This solution helps us.)

3. Last, your own needs.
   (This solution helps me.)

The Roundtrip Leads to a Real Connection

You can talk about the situation in two ways. Here is the straight line that will invite opposition: "I am serving on the committee and heard that you are too. I look forward to working with you." Here is the Roundtrip toward rapport. "I have heard that you are an expert in this area, so you might be interested in an idea to help the committee gain support more quickly. I'd like to describe it to you. By serving on this committee with you, I know I'll gain valuable experience to take back to my group. Should I describe the idea briefly now or wait until another time?"

> Whoever most vividly describes a situation usually determines how others see it, feel about it, and act upon it.

When you use the Roundtrip to reach solutions, other people will start listening sooner, pay more attention, listen for a longer time, and remember more of what you say. They will assume that you are intelligent and have more respect for you. They therefore will give you more latitude and listen more closely when you talk about your own needs.

Show how your ideas are close to the ideas, desires, or values of the other side. If necessary, find a part of the other side's values or self-image that you share. Admire it and refer to it frequently.

People always feel more comfortable when a precedent in attitude has been set. When there's a laughtrack on a TV show, people will believe the show is funny, even though they don't like laughtracks. Change is less difficult, less threatening to people when others they admire have gone through the same change, when people in authority endorse the idea, when they believe that you like them or are like them, when you appeal to the best image they have of themselves, in relation to the proposal.

> Quiet the chattering mind to promote directed action.

Position Yourself

When you position your suggestions, first for their benefit, than for both of your benefits, then with your benefit, you accomplish four things.

1. You show people what's in it for them.
2. You let them know you are committed to collaboration, not competition.
3. You show them that your intentions are honorable.
4. You shift their attention toward the opportunities your proposal affords.

Build bridges between your side and theirs by addressing their interests and then demonstrating how they relate to yours. Refer to others who have already done what you are proposing.

Make the opportunity more vivid than the risk. People are often more afraid of negative possibilities than the positive ones, even if the positive factors outweigh the negatives in the number of risks or degree of risk. Whoever most vividly characterizes a situation usually determines how others think about it, talk about it, and make decisions about it.

Give a point away without being asked to do so. People will open up and instinctively want to reciprocate, to give you something in return. Your early generosity encourages the same in others.

How to Deal with Bad News

When you must be the bearer of bad news and want to avoid being tainted by it, create a nonstick coating that will protect you. When you have to discuss a negative issue, first point out something in it that is genuinely positive, offer related information that is negative, and immediately point out more positive information. Help people feel safe by beginning and ending your speech positively. Sandwich bad news between good news.

Determine the Focus of Attention

Consider which points you want to emphasize. This will steer people's perceptions of your request. Make some words or phrases especially vivid. For instance, Peggy Noonan made George Bush's campaign memorable when she wrote for him such phrases as, "Read my lips."

When you praise specific qualities of other people, make sure you associate those qualities with yourself. Compliments stick.

You have an opportunity to shine and also dissipate criticism when you genuinely praise others after they have directly or indirectly criticized you. Like good product positioning, the contrast is sharp, between you and them.

If one person has been critical of you in the past, he will probably criticize you again. Plan ahead to find a quality in him that you can genuinely praise. Decline the opportunity to escalate the conflict. Whenever you throw mud, you get dirty.

When you plan to make an offer that will invite opposition, describe the other, less attractive possibilities first, and then explain your offer. It will look more attractive in contrast.

In conflict, we tend to make things worse by remembering the best of our own actions and the worst of the other person's.

Describe the most expensive option first to convince the other person that they don't want to settle for less. For example, when a man enters a store prepared to buy a suit for two hundred and fifty dollars, a smart salesperson will hand him three suits to try on. The first suit to try on is priced at eight hundred dollars, the second at five hundred dollars, the third at two hundred and fifty dollars. The first Italian suit looks great, the second okay.

By the time the man sees himself in the mirror in a two hundred and fifty dollar suit, he will decide he doesn't want it, that it's worth it to pay more for the suit he really wants. When you describe the options, you often determine the selection.

Instead of offering only one option, offer two, either of which will help move you toward agreement. Giving the other person only one option gives them no choice at all. By offering them two, you will please them, and it is more likely they will help you continue the momentum toward agreement.

> Help people feel safe and positive by beginning and ending your interaction positively.

Stay Calm

When the going gets tough, when you are down to the wire when all parties must finally decide what to do, it's time to deactivate your own hot buttons and stay calm. This is hardest and most crucial when you're determining the final agreement. Do try to remember that the conflict is really no one's fault, neither yours, nor the other person's. You'll have more self-control when you stay clear about your main need. Air your differences without blame or coercion. To avoid letting positions harden, do the following:

1. Decrease the amount of direct interaction in the early stages of discussion.
2. Decrease the amount of time between problem-solving sessions.
3. Decrease formality.
4. Limit how widely and how far back precedents can be cited.
5. Use objective third parties as mediators.

You Always Have Three Choices

In this situation or really in any situation, there are always three alternatives.

1. You can accept the situation as it is.
2. You can change your behavior.
3. You can walk out.

You will feel most stressed and reactive before you make your decision. Before you do, ask yourself what you can learn from the situation. This may help you see the scene as positive, rather than negative. You might not like the situation any better after you make your choice, but you will have learned something new about yourself and the other side.

When both sides are stuck and not able to reach agreement, look to the other side's positive intent. Your willingness to do this may make the others more likely to act in a more positive way. Fight your instinct to talk first. Don't talk a lot. Don't talk about what you don't like or want to improve or correct.

It may be useful instead to speak directly to the other person to see if there's any chance of reaching agreement. Keep the positive big picture especially in your mind, particularly at this time when the current picture upsets you.

Differences Between Men and Women

This may be the time to look at the causes of conflict between men and women. In general, women want to build rapport, whereas men are trained to win. Men tend to stuff their feelings and therefore remain angry longer. Women tend to express their feelings and forgive and forget more quickly. Both women and men want to feel liked and respected. However, it's more important to women that they are liked, whereas men desire respect most. Consequently their ways of resolving conflict may be different.

A person who is successful at resolving conflicts has both qualities: empathy and the ability to set boundaries. The female quality is empathy, the ability to sense another's needs and talk about them. The male quality is understanding one's own needs first and maintaining boundaries without getting sidetracked by someone else's needs. In an ideal world, women could learn to set clearer boundaries and men could loosen them.

What If You Walk Out?

When the hassle of trying to reach agreement seems overwhelming, consider the amount of effort you'd have to expend if you walked out. And, if the other person feels similarly frustrated, you might ask them the same question.

> What you most vividly emphasize is what others most remember.

You might acknowledge your frustration publicly and say if we can stick it out we'll have something to show for our effort. Take time out for five minutes to review out loud whatever progress has been made.

You can also see if you personally can change in some way that can improve the situation. Remember, you are the part of the conflict over which you have the most control.

What Can You Do?

1. Pinpoint what's happening.
2. Analyze what needs to happen to get things going.
3. Change your own behavior accordingly.

4. Evaluate how the attempt to correct your behavior is working.

How to Deal with Difficulties

The more people who participate in the problem-solving process, the more they will like you, themselves, and the solution you propose. You can ask for their opinions frequently, invite them to be part of a committee or do some needed research. You can ask everybody to participate in discussions. You can pick out the individuals you think least responsive and sit near them. Don't let the other person feel isolated. This statement will help: "We all want to come away winners."

> Shut people out and
> they shut up.
> Bring people in and they
> open up.

When there isn't much cooperation from the other person, become even more courteous, a valuable tactic when they are vicious. However, be clear about what you will or will not tolerate. Don't waffle, stick to what you say. Be clear about your boundaries—it's a way of showing respect for yourself and for the other side.

When an argument lasts longer than ten minutes, ask yourself whether there's a deeper, hidden issue. Do anything to change the energy. Bring someone new into the discussion, change the subject, shift your location, or finally take a break. Disrupt the flow in order to stop the escalation in conflict.

When you're wrong, admit it quickly, apologize to the people most affected, and make clear what you are going to do differently. People will respect you for your courage.

You don't have to fight every battle or respond immediately to every inquiry. When you aren't ready to respond or would prefer not to give a response at all, acknowledge what the other person has said, but don't agree with that person. Simply say, "You might have a point," or "That could be true," two good ways of fogging the scene. Choose your battles by merely acknowledging inquiries.

Some people will sideswipe you by pretending to be joking when they are making nasty comments. It's foolish to confront such slurs directly—it's far wiser to disarm them by acting that they were indeed kidding you, that the joke is excellent. You will look better while the other person will look worse.

When someone won't give others a chance to participate, wait for a pause in his monologue, acknowledge
his comments, and then turn to another person and ask
for their view. Shifting your attention from the most
talkative person to the least talkative one opens up the
conversation to everyone present.

Share Power

People in a group operate best when they feel the power
is shared. If you are perceived as having more power than
the other person and offer no compensation, they will
resist you out of pride. Find ways to let the other side
assume more power.

On the other hand, if you have less power, act as
though your power is equal to the other person and
the relationship may balance out.

Pinpoint the specific sources of your power so you
can use it more efficiently. Positional power stems from
your role in society. Personal power comes from intan-
gible things—how you present yourself, how much
information you have, etc. Other sources of power
come from good looks, likeability, verbal ability, experience, knowledge, etc.

Emotionally laden language is just another way we
throw our power around. Avoid phrases such as these:

- "Let's be fair." (translated, I want you to play by my rules.)
- "Can you prove that?" (translated, I know you can't, but it will be fun watching you try.)
- "You don't really mean that." (translated, I know you better than you know yourself.)
- "What you really mean is..." (translated, I am smarter than you and will tell you what you mean, or, You are kidding me.)
- "Where did you get that idea?" (translated, How stupid are you?)
- "I'll get to that later." (translated, Shut up and let me handle this.)

Such tactics always backfire. You will seem trivial if you resort to stuff like this.

When you describe the options, you often determine the selection.

Most people underestimate their own power and sometimes assume they have a weaker position than they really do.

Do claim your power by doing the following:

1. Find out what the real driving force is behind your bottom line in this conflict.

2. Rank your wants in order of importance.

3. Determine who or what stands in your way.

4. Identify your resources.

5. Choose the timing so that you can use your power best.

Suggesting the choices often speeds selection.

Ten Approaches for Offering Your Solution

1. Picture Each Person Benefiting in Some Way.

You have come up with a proposal you think is fair to all parties and have shaped your offer so that everyone will see it in the best light possible. Before you speak about your own needs, you have addressed their needs first and worked through whatever obstacles or power issues that have surfaced.

Now it's time to make an offer. You hope that it will be accepted quickly without fuss. However, in the real world even the best proposal won't go through if it is presented in a way people can't accept. Your manner of presenting your proposal will be more important than its solid core. There are surefire ways to sabotage a good offer.

- Present it with open contempt for the other side.
- Give in to your fear that it won't be accepted.

- Act in anger or with animosity.
- Bully others or play king of the mountain.

According to Abraham Maslow, "People take action in order to satisfy essential human needs."

2. Don't Talk Before You Are Prepared to Reach Agreement

If you start talking with the other person before you are ready to reach an agreement you could wind up with less than you want. Be sure

> Everyone needs to feel heard before they'll listen.

- You have gotten what you want out of the situation (Step One).
- The other person has felt heard.
- You are emotionally ready to settle.
- Check your heart and your mind before you open your mouth to seek closure to the conflict.

3. Demonstrate Continued Good Will

At the beginning of conflict, we look for signals from others that tell us how they will act. Later we use these signals as a screen through which we view their actions.

Because first impressions make the strongest impact. So when presenting your proposal, make sure your initial tone, gestures, and language show that you have good intentions. Succeeding impressions are not so important. New, different information about what someone is like is often disregarded.

Continue to be congenial, specifically because this could be the state when you get more impatient, restless, or judgmental as you become tired of the process and the other side. You might try to

- Minimize your defensiveness.
- Bring out the other's better sides.
- Orient yourself so that you will look for the other side's more positive traits.
- Demonstrate your own best traits.

People are more inclined to be willing to resolve a conflict with someone they consider fair than with someone they like, but don't trust.

4. Don't Bluff

Bluffing can harm you in two ways. It can stick you with an agreement that doesn't meet your bottom line, and it can undermine your credibility.

5. If You Think Your Part of the Pie Is Too Small, Picture a Larger Pie

If you don't like the alternative solutions, step back and look at a bigger picture. Ask yourself what is at stake for everyone. Ask yourself whether either of you has more to offer, or whether a different combination of actions could make your solution more fair to the other person. By doing so, you might see ways to keep the provisions of your offer intact, but arrange them differently to increase parity. If you can see a bigger picture of the people involved including their lives, you may find more options.

6. Use the Pressure of Time to Increase Effectiveness

It's a good idea to demonstrate your ability to be graceful under pressure. People will admire you for this. Never exhibit any panic—it wastes time and eliminates any chance for clarity. As an aside, it may be fruitful to remember that the pressure of time might be greater for the other person than you assume. The more pressured you feel, the more important it is to look relaxed.

7. Don't Leave Your Most Important Points for Last

Don't raise your important points at the beginning of the discussion, nor at the end of the discussion. Waiting until the end can close off some of the best options for trade-offs. Reach agreement on your key items before you make any gesture toward finalizing agreement. When the other side avoids discussion of their most important needs, their avoidance will eventually impede progress toward resolution.

8. Ask Another, Mutually Respected Person to Mediate When Necessary

A fair and neutral witness can make everyone involved in a conflict feel safer and more heard, especially when it's necessary to review items over which you have become deadlocked. This person may be a friend, colleague, or a professional mediator. It doesn't matter as long as the person chosen by both sides has the training and strength of character to stay focused on the solution, whether you are using the Roundtrip or another approach.

> The more opportunities you provide for others to participate in a situation along the way, the more likely they will stay with you to find a solution.

It's also wise to have a third party act as witness to your final agreement. It's an extra bit of insurance—sometimes the other side may not live up to the agreement, and if there is a witness, it's harder to avoid making commitments.

9. Stay Flexible

Be, and appear to be, flexible to keep the momentum going towards a resolution. This flexibility also will restore the momentum where you have gotten off track.

Observe how the others are reacting to you and your proposal.

Stay flexible so that you can correct yourself and shift gears to make the situation feel safer and more fair.

Open-ended questions open people up.

If feelings seem to be escalating or the other person appears to be shutting down, ask for suggestions and express your willingness to look at other options.

If you appear to grow more rigid, even if the other person is doing it too, the others will become wary, suspicious of all your future suggestions.

10. Honor Everyone Else's Role in Coming to Terms

It's important to acknowledge the participation of others.

- Listen and thoroughly consider other people's opinions at the moment they are presented. If you disagree immediately or counter with another suggestion, reactions will remain hardened long after this particular discussion.

- Acknowledge the respect you feel for the others involved.

- Speak to the relationship you have built.

- Mention that you respect the people who are important to the other side.

- Praise specific contributions the others have made and let them know you appreciate their efforts.

- Make sure that the other side will share your satisfaction in coming to agreement. It's very important that the resolution appears to be arrived at together.

Reach a Solid Closure

After you complete the four Roundtrip steps and resolve the conflict, make sure it feels concrete to all the people involved. You might want to relax and move on to other matters since there seems to be a resolution on the table. Don't relax—make absolutely sure the agreement is clear to all sides. This is the time when uncertainty and loose ends become obvious. These must be cleared up before you proceed. Don't be afraid to clarify and confirm.

Never nibble at the pact, seeking further concessions after the agreement is made. And don't let the other side nibble at it either. Car salesmen sometimes use this technique after reaching an agreement. If you attempt to change even one tiny aspect of the agreement, you will lose others' trust and respect and moreover leave yourself open to any attempt to renegotiate the agreement you have worked so hard to put on the table.

1. Prepare a Written Agreement

Even when the agreement is among friends or family, or especially so in this case, quietly insist on putting the agreement in writing. This will preserve the relationship and the agreement. Offer to take on the task of making a draft for everyone involved to review. Write down the agreement as soon as possible after you reach it while the details are fresh in everyone's mind. Offer to write it down on the spot. Write it accurately, so that you will not have to repeat the battle, and can focus on fostering the relationship.

Keep cool under fire by keeping your bottom line on top of your mind.

However simple or complex the agreement is, the words on paper will act as a shared reality for future reference. Good fences make good neighbors. When boundaries are concrete, it's easier for both sides to adjust.

2. Debrief with People Whom You Trust

After an agreement is made, we instinctively recall our successes more clearly than our mistakes. A year after giving birth, a woman will recall the joy more clearly than the pain. In this case, it's smarter to scan the path towards resolution objectively. It means you will be better able to master future conflicts and you will at the same time become a bigger, better person.

Review where you most need improvement.

> "The opposite of a fact is a falsehood, but the opposite of one profound truth may very well be another profound truth."
>
> *Niels Bohr, physicist*

- Ask for honest feedback from people you trust as to what you could have done better to help yourself and the other side in the conflict.

- Review your best achievements in the conflict.

- Celebrate.

- Honest feedback, compassionately given, honors everyone.

3. Do What You Said You Would Do, and Then Some

If you are able to resolve conflicts and make and keep agreements, it will be one of your enduring strengths, attracting and deepening genuine relationships. Incidentally, how you respond to conflict will give people greater insight into your character than how you respond to respect or adoration. You never really know someone until you see the choices that he makes, and the most revealing choices are the ones made in times of disagreement.

Match your words with your actions in order to build trust. Practice Roundtrips until they become second nature. People will instinctively trust you, a vital resource when something goes awry. And as you grow more reliable, people are less inclined to escalate when they disagree with you.

4. Make Good Agreements a Way of Life

Why should you make Roundtrips a regular habit? What's in it for you?

- You will be more adept when you have to resolve big conflicts in any part of your life, and you will reach better agreements more easily.

- You will be more open to the way other people perceive life; therefore, you will have more options in problem solving and will reach better agreements more easily.

- You will stay centered because you will keep your higher vision of yourself more clearly in your conscience.

- You will become a more open and a more powerful person.

- You will let go of beliefs and habits that limit you.

- Your life will expand with new levels of personal satisfaction, effectiveness, and confidence.

It will help if you make an agreement with a close friend that you will support each other in practicing Roundtrips.

- Discuss each other's anticipated Roundtrips to visualize and practice a positive outcome.

- Share reactions to the tips in this book.

- Use one another as consultants when either one of you is in the midst of a conflict.

- Use Roundtrips when you have a conflict with each other. Be sure to debrief each other after you have reached resolution.

Problems seldom exist at the level at which they are expressed. Share power.

Soon the steps will become second nature, a habit. Choose three tips and make a resolution to practice them over the next six months. Write down what you choose to begin practicing right now, then next week. Do a six-month review. Set a date now for that review.

Move to the Next Level: Mastery at Making and Keeping Agreements

1. Start with Small Steps

Give yourself a break. Learn to improve situations where small, easier to make changes in your behavior can improve your life. Note which of the four Roundtrip steps you find hardest and easiest to adopt. Build momentum and savor small successes. Then move to the most toxic conflict-laden situations where you are most resistant to changing how you choose to react.

How do you recognize these situations? By the way you feel? When you feel most wounded, you are in a conflict-laden situation. The deepest, most long-lasting wounds come when someone has either left you or attacked you. A person may leave you by ignoring your presence and comments as well as literally going away from you. A person may attack you or your comments verbally as well as physically.

Until you have attained some mastery with Roundtrips, avoid or minimize contact with people who exhibit patterns that appear at all similar to similar behaviors that affected you strongly when you were a child. Protect yourself until you gain confidence by practicing the Roundtrips. These are the hardest lessons you will encounter.

2. Lighten Up

When other people begin to show some heat, we either escalate or withdraw. We either become like them and get louder and more hostile, or mimic them in other ways. Or we put on a poker face and withdraw. Either approach gets us off center. Both approaches are ways of protecting ourselves and sabotaging ourselves. In essence, what we are saying is, "I don't like your behavior—therefore, I am giving you more power." Instead, slow everything down: your voice level, the speed at which you speak, and the number and frequency of your body motions.

Be aware of yourself and rather than dwelling on your anger, move to de-escalate and leave room for everyone, especially the person in the wrong, to save face and self-correct.

3. Take the Four "A" Approach to Agreement

- **Acknowledge** that you have heard the person and then pause. This buys time for both people to cool off. Give a nod or say something that indicates you have heard the person. You should not immediately take sides. Your approach should be, "I understand you have a concern," rather than "You shouldn't have…" There should be no blaming at this point. The thrust is "Let's discuss what would work best for us both now," rather than "That was dumb…" Don't use language that provokes the other person to become more hardened in her position.

  > Contrary to common belief, most disagreements are caused not by conflict over what people need but by how they actually talk and act about those needs.

- **Ask** for more information. It's a way you both can cool off so that you can possibly find some common ground based on the other person's underlying concerns or needs. Try to focus on that part of the person you respect. Then refer to it verbally. For instance, "You are so dedicated (knowledgeable)."

- **Agree** with the part of what they said with which you feel a genuine connection.

- **Add** your own perspective, but ask permission first. Say perhaps, "May I tell you my perspective?"

4. Presume Innocence

Nobody wants to be told they are wrong. If you have reason to believe someone is lying or not making sense, you will not build rapport by pointing it out to them. Allow them to save face and keep asking questions. Say, "How does that relate to the issue?" and explore the apparently conflicting information.

It's possible you were wrong—this will enable you to save face. Or through continuing nonthreatening questions, you can softly corner the other person into correcting himself. This procedure protects your future relationship.

> Keep a positive "big picture," especially when the current picture upsets you.

5. Look to Others' Positive Intent, Especially When They Appear to Have None

Our instinct is to look for the ways we are right and the other party wrong. As the momentum of the argument builds, we mentally focus on the smart, thoughtful, and right things we are doing, while obsessing about the dumb, thoughtless, and otherwise wrong things the other party is doing. This tends to more rigidity and less listening, to more righteous position building.

Difficult as it may be when you are drawn into an escalating argument, try to stay mindful of where you are worst and where the other party is best. You will then be more generous and patient and increase the possibility that they will see areas where you might be right after all.

6. Dump Their Stuff Back in Their Laps

If someone is verbally dumping on you, do not interrupt, counter, or counterattack in their midstream. You will only prolong and intensify their comments. When they finish, ask, "Do you want to add anything else?" Then ask, "What would make this situation better?" or "How can we improve this situation in a way we can both accept?"

Then ask them to propose a solution to the issue they have raised. If they continue to complain or attack, simply acknowledge you have heard them, and if necessary, repeat yourself again and again, in fewer and fewer words, "What will make it better?"

Do not attempt to solve problems others raise, even if they ask for advice. They won't hear you. People tend to prove that their way works better, rather than accepting a method suggested by someone else, even if that someone is someone they love or like. It's only human.

7. Learn How Personalities Clash

Would you like some insights as to why you often get into conflict with some people, whereas you don't with others? You could take a Myers-Briggs test from a specialist, as an accurate way to get a readout on your patterns. Or take a free sampler test on the Internet. Here are two places where you can take an abbreviated version of the test and read about what happens when different types interact:

http://www.whitman.edu/peterscc/psych/jung.html
http://www.keirsey.com/cgi-bin/keirsey/newkts.cgi

8. Demonstrate Good Will Up Front

Establish your willingness to find a compromise. Establish the fact that you are genial, even (and especially) if you don't like the person or situation. This should be principally a commitment to your own standard of behavior; it also happens to be the best way to keep the channels open.

9. Know that Less Is Often More

Listen more, talk less, move less. Keep your motions slower, your voice lower and slower. These actions are especially effective in the beginning—others will feel more safe and comfortable around you—you will not appear to be a threatening animal.

10. Honor Commonality More Frequently than Differences

Keep referring to what you can support and want to expand on in the other person's agenda and character. Whatever you refer to most often and most intensely becomes the center of your relationship.

11. Agree among Yourselves First

If there is another person(s) on your "side," even though you both know the content to be discussed, the other person may not know your bottom line. Establish this first.

Even your genial colleague may not hear the same thing you hear. Review your bottom line and specific approach before you enter discussion with the other side.

> To fight fair, women could set clearer boundaries and men could loosen their boundaries.

12. Choose a Safe Spokesperson

Have a point person if several of you are involved on one side of the conflict. One should always be responsible in taking the lead in discussion.

13. Let the Other Person See the Situation Differently

Try stating your initial suggestion another way. Rearrange the elements of the same suggestion or offer to find a more attractive compromise. For example, consider alternative timing or spaced increments of payments of money.

You are the part of the conflict over which you have the most control.

14. Don't Get Your Hopes Dashed by Getting Distracted

You have to be present to win. Keep grounded, involved in what is happening right now, glancing to the past and future only for context and balance.

15. Choose Your Approach

Contemplate how to say what you say. Consider the other person's perspective before you make *any* request. For example, a priest once asked his superior if he could smoke while praying. His request was denied. He would have received permission had he asked if he could pray while smoking.

16. Be Fair

It's more important to be fair, rather than well liked. These attributes are not mutually exclusive, but are not always the same.

17. R-E-S-P-E-C-T Your Method

Even if you can't respect the person, always show respect for your process. If you embarrass someone when you are trying to reach agreement, you may never have their full attention again.

18. R-E-S-P-E-C-T Yourself

By respecting others, you show respect for yourself. Whenever you have the upper hand, do not make a victim of the underdog.

19. Remember Trust Instills Trust.

20. Describe the Common Ground Under You All

Be a "synthesizer" leader, using some of their comments as your starting place. The person who listens longest at first and then refers to the other side's earlier points as a way of framing a proposed solution usually attracts positive power, especially in a rancorous situation.

21. Help Them Like Themselves

Support them in liking how they are acting. The more they like the way they are when they are around you, the greater the chances they will like you. They might even give you credit for things you did not do and go out of the way to help you, sometimes to their own detriment. On the other hand, if they do not like the way they are when they are around you, they will blame you for it more than they are consciously aware. They won't give you credit for things you did and might sabotage projects on which you are working—even to their own detriment.

22. Ask How We Will Live With It

Show them the positive, longer view. Many seemingly foolish disagreements are simply actions to prevent looking foolish later on. The best peacemakers work hardest to allay the other person's worries first.

23. Help Them Change

People change most easily when they believe others they respect have already done something similar. Third-party endorsements from those other people are a credible grounding for your points.

24. Offer the Overpoweringly Alluring Possibility of Peace

Paint your biggest, best picture for others. Give people a vivid picture of all they could have, and they often won't settle for the lesser option they originally considered.

25. Look for the Real Source of the Anger

When someone is angry with you, consider that she might be upset with herself before you respond.

26. Aim Humor at Yourself

One way to release tension is to poke fun at yourself. Make reference to a situation when you did something foolish.

Tool Kit for Putting Roundtrips into Practice

Look Inside Yourself

Step One: Truth-Taking, tell yourself what you most want out of the situation.

Look at The Situation as They See It

Step Two: Receiving, reach out to find out what others want and let them feel heard.

Prove You've Looked at It from Their Perspective

Step Three: Involving, invite openness so others want to stick in to seek resolution.

Suggest a Solution that Shows Their Benefits

Step Four: Proposing, prove fairness by Discussing Their Interests First

Propose a Solution

Forge an Agreement

The Mini-Roundtrip To Resolving Conflict:
Going around from you to the other person, and back to you for a solution

1. "Me—My Bottom Line"
   Be very specific about your main need in the situation.

2. "You—the Possibility of Your Bottom Line"
   Contemplate the other person's greatest need, as she/he sees the situation.

3. "You—the Confirmation of Your Bottom Line, Proving Fair Intent"
   Discover what the other person really sees as his/her main need, proving that you care to be fair, as you seek that vital insight.

4. "Me—Proposing a Fair Solution"
   Characterize their main need, next your common ground of interests, your proposed solution to meet both your main needs.

Handy Checklist of 100+ Ways of Resolving Conflict Sooner

1. Resolving Conflict Requires Reaching for Connection
2. How Conflict Escalates to the Point of No Return
3. How You Can Take a "Roundtrip" to Resolution
4. Why Roundtrips Work
5. Roundtrips, Your "Visual Trigger" Reminder
6. Ten Payoffs to Taking Roundtrips
7. Take a Roundtrip to Avoid Conflict-Increasing Traps
8. Identifying Your Main Truth So You Can Establish Your Bottom-Line Need
9. Make "What Do I Want?" an Automatic Response
10. How Our Survival Instinct Works Against Us
11. Consider Alternatives, and Choose One
12. Create a Vivid, One-Sentence Mental Image of What You Most Want

Handy Checklist continued

13. Know Yourself and What Is Most Important to You
14. Know How Others See You
15. Understand Your Situational Patterns and Sources of Positive Power
16. Probe for Others' Needs
17. The Defensive Driving Look Ahead Rule
18. Find Out What Others' Words and Behaviors Mean
19. Recognize Your Own—and Others'—Greatest Fears
20. When You're Talking to the Opposite Sex
21. Don't Assume You Know What Someone Else Wants
22. See the World the Way Others Do
23. Allow for Others' Lack of Self-Awareness
24. People Like People Who Like Them
25. Allow Time Up Front to Get in Sync
26. People Like People Who Are Like Them
27. Expect the Best of Yourself and Others
28. Cast a Wide Net with Initial Questions
29. Move from the Oblique to the Specific
30. Ask Advice and Send Up Trial Balloons
31. Show You're Really Listening
32. Avoid Being King of the Mountain

Handy Checklist continued

33. Act As If Others Mean Well
34. Ask Direct Questions
35. Accept the Situation As It Is
36. Don't Let Emotions Sabotage Your Attempt to Forge Agreement
37. Create a Bridge, Not a Gulf, When Emotions Are Hot
38. Acknowledge Others' Concerns
39. Use Others' Language and Points of Reference
40. Give Yourself a Progress Report
41. Speak to Others' Interests First
42. Roundtrip to Real Connection
43. Position Yourself and Your Ideas to Build Bridges and Shape Perceptions
44. Paint a Colorful, Alluring Picture
45. Give Something Away Without Being Asked
46. Sandwich Bad News Between Good
47. Determine the Focus of Attention
48. Lavish Velcro Praise on Others
49. Influence Others' Choices by How You Describe the Alternatives
50. Suggest Two Alternatives to Get One
51. Make Your Offer Desirable by Making It Scarce

Handy Checklist continued

52. Overcome Obstacles When the Going Gets Tough
53. Stay Open When You Feel Like Closing Down
54. Remember Your Three Choices
55. Emphasize Others' Best Qualities
56. Men Organize to Solve; Women Empathize to Connect
57. Show the Disadvantages of Quitting Versus the Benefits of Continuing
58. Give All Participants a Stake in the Outcome
59. Be Courteous, Respectful, and Clear
60. Use the Ten-Minute Rule
61. Admit You're Wrong Before Others Do
62. "Fog" to Avoid or Postpone a Response
63. Employ the Messy Desk Solution
64. Shift the Spotlight
65. Empower, Don't Coerce
66. Speak Fairly
67. Take the Power You Need
68. Picture Each Person Benefiting in Some Way
69. Don't Talk Before You're Prepared to Reach Agreement
70. Demonstrate Continued Good Will
71. Don't Bluff

Handy Checklist continued

72. If You Think Your Part of the Pie Is Too Small, Picture a Larger Pie

73. Use the Time Pressure to Increase Effectiveness

74. Don't Leave Your Most Important Points for Last

75. Ask Another, Mutually Respected Person to Mediate When Necessary

76. Stay Flexible

77. Honor Others' Roles in Coming to Terms

78. Reach a Solid Closure

79. Prepare a Written Agreement

80. Debrief with Those You Trust

81. Do What You Said You Would Do and Then Some

82. Make Good Agreements a Way of Life

83. Start with Small Steps

84. Lighten Up

85. Use the Four A's to Approaching Agreement

86. Presume Innocence

87. Look to Others' Positive Intent, Especially When They Appear to Have None

88. Dump Their Stuff Back in Their Laps

89. Ask What Will Make it Better

90. Learn How Personalities Clash

Handy Checklist continued

91. Demonstrate Visible Good Will Up Front
92. Know Less is Often More
93. Act to Enable Others to Save Face, and You Will Preserve the Relationship
94. Honor Commonality More Frequently Than You Bring Up Differences
95. Choose a Safe Spokesperson
96. Let Them See It Differently
97. Don't Get Your Hopes Dashed by Getting Distracted
98. Choose Your Approach
99. Find Fairness First
100. Agree Among Yourselves First
101. R-E-S-P-E-C-T Your Method
102. R-E-S-P-E-C-T Yourself
103. Remember Trust Instills Trust
104. Describe the Common Ground Under You All
105. Help Them Like Themselves
106. Ask How We Will Live With It
107. Help Them Change
108. Offer the Overpoweringly Alluring Possibility of Peace
109. Look for the Real Source of the Anger
110. Aim Humor at Yourself

Suggested Reading

The Argument Culture: Moving from Debate to Dialogue
  by Deborah Tannen

Art of Resolving Conflict in the Workplace
  by Lawrence Schwimmer

Beloved Enemies: Our Need for Opponents
  by David P. Barash

Betting to Yes: Negotiation Agreement Without Giving In
  by Roger Fisher and William Ury

Beyond Blame: A New Way of Resolving Conflicts in Relationships
  by Jeffrey A. Kottler

Changing the World One Relationship at a Time
  by Sheryl Karas

Conflict Management: A Communication Skills Approach
  by Deborah Borisoff and David A. Victor

Conscious Marriage
  by John C. Lucas, Ph.D.

Suggested Reading continued

*Creating Balance: Moving Out of Conflict
into Compatibility*
    by Carolyn Dickson

*The Dance of Anger: A Woman's Guide to Changing
the Patterns of Intimate Relationships*
    by Harriet Goldhor Lerner

*The Dance of Intimacy: A Woman's Guide to
Courageous Acts of Change in Key Relationships*
    by Harriet Goldhor Lerner

Dealing With Fighting
    by Marianne Johnston

*The Delicate Art of Dancing With Porcupines:
Learning to Appreciate the Finer Points of Others*
    by Bob Phillips

*Family Mediation: Managing Conflict,
Resolving Disputes*
    by Robert Coulson

*Getting What You Want: Resolving Conflict and
Winning Agreement Every Time*
    by Kare Anderson

How to Bring Out the Best in People at Their Worst
    by Dr. Rick Brinkman

How to Get What You Want from Almost Anybody
    by T. Scott Bross

Suggested Reading continued

If Only I'd Listen to Myself: Resolving the Conflicts That Sabotage Our Lives
by Jacques Salome and Sylvie Galland

Influence: The Psychology of Persuasion
by Robert B. Cialdini

Mastery: The Keys to Success and Long-Term Fulfillment
by George Leonard

Plant Your Feet Firmly in Mid-Air: Guidance Through Turbulent Change
by Dr. Janet Lapp

The Platinum Rule
by Tony Alessandra

The Power Principle: Influence with Honor
by Stephen R. Covey

Resolving Conflict: A Practical Approach
by Gregory Tillett

Resolving Conflicts: How to Turn Conflict into Cooperation
by Wendy Grant

Resolving Conflict: Learning How You Both Can Win and Keep Your Relationship
by Dale R. Olen

Resolving Conflict With Others and Within Yourself
by Gina Graham Scott

Suggested Reading continued

Students Resolving Conflict: Peer Mediation in Schools
  by Richard Cohen

Teambuilt: Making Teamwork Work
  by Mark Sanborn

Tongue Fu!: How to Deflect, Disarm, and Defuse Any Verbal Conflict
  by Sam Horn

When You and Your Mother Can't Be Friends: Resolving the Most Complicated Relationship of Your Life
  by Victoria Secunda

Win/Win Solutions: Resolving Conflict on the Job
  by Thomas J. Stevinin

❋ THE CROSSING PRESS, INC.

For a catalog of our books, contact us at:
TEL: 800-777-1048   FAX: 800-549-0020

www.crossingpress.com